Science

Was the Bible Ahead of Its Time?

Ralph O. Muncaster

HARVEST HOUSE PUBLISHERS
Eugene, Oregon 97402

A SPECIAL THANKS . . .

. . . To Mark Ritter for his technical editing assistance. Mark holds B.S. and M.S. degrees from California State Polytechnic University, Pomona, with emphasis in chemistry and mathematics. He has taught various courses in science including chemistry and astronomy. Mark is an apologetics correspondent for Reasons To Believe, an organization devoted to examining the scientific accuracy of the Bible (see notes and bibliography on page 48). He is also president and editor of Sword and Spirit ministry.

By Ralph O. Muncaster

Are There Contradictions in The Bible?
Can Archaeology Prove the New Testament?
Can Archaeology Prove the Old Testament?
Can We Know for Certain We Are Going To Heaven?
Can You Trust The Bible?
Creation vs. Evolution
Does Prayer Really Work?
Does the Bible Predict the Future?
How Do We Know Jesus Is God?
How is Jesus Different from Other Religious Leaders?
How to Talk About Jesus With the Skeptics in Your Life
Is The Bible Really A Message From God?
Science—Was the Bible Ahead of It's Time?
What is the Proof For the Resurrection?
What is the Trinity?
What Really Happened Christmas Morning?
What Really Happens When You Die?
Why Are Scientists Turning to God?
Why Does God Allow Suffering?

Cover by Terry Dugan Design, Minneapolis, Minnesota

SCIENCE—WAS THE BIBLE AHEAD OF ITS TIME?
Copyright © 2000 by Ralph O. Muncaster
Published by Harvest House Publishers
Eugene, Oregon 97402

Library of Congress Cataloging-in-Publication Data

Muncaster, Ralph O.
    Science—was the bible ahead of its time? / Ralph O. Muncaster.
        p. cm. — (Examine the evidence series)
    Includes bibliographical references.
    ISBN 0-7369-0354-2
        1. Bible and science. 2. Bible—Evidences, authority, etc. I. Title.

BS650 .M86 2000
220.8'8—dc21   00-024159

Printed in the United States of America.

02 03 04 05 06 07 08 09 / BP / 10 9 8 7 6 5 4 3

Contents

Suppose Science Supports the Bible 4

The Key Issues 6

How the Bible Fits with History 8

An Overview of the Bible Relative to Science 10

Why Science Seems at Odds with the Bible 18

Evidence for Creation 20

The Creation Events of Genesis 1 22

Historical Comparison of Scientific Insights 24

Insights into Medicine 26

Insights into Biology and Chemistry 30

Insights into Engineering and Agriculture 32

Insights into Physics 34

Insights into Physics—Twentieth Century Discoveries 36

Insights into Astronomy 38

Insights into Geology 40

Understanding Miracles 42

Common Questions About Bible Events 44

Other Common Questions 46

Notes 48

Bibliography 48

Suppose Science Supports the Bible . . .

Many people think that science and the Bible are at odds. This notion causes some of them to reject the Bible without investigating the facts.

Suppose the latest scientific findings actually verified that the Bible has been accurate all along—even to the smallest detail? Wouldn't it be incredible if biblical authors thousands of years ago had received information that escaped even Newton, Galileo, and Pasteur? Wouldn't it be amazing if insights—which require particle accelerators, space probes, and electron microscopes for human beings to discover—were accurately recorded centuries before Christ? All this would seem to support the claim that information was supernaturally given to biblical authors by God. And if the Bible really is God's attempt to communicate to us— then it would be foolish not to be interested in it because:

- the Bible promises eternal life to anyone willing to take a few simple steps.

- the Bible promises strength to face any challenges on a daily basis.

- the Bible promises joy on earth and forever.

Skeptics and atheists who are aware of the latest breakthroughs in science are now being forced to reconsider their doubts about the Bible. And many of today's most prominent scientists are for the first time considering—literally—the *probability of the God of the Bible*.

News that affects beliefs about God seems to travel slowly. Even though the importance of these new findings is stressed by such prominent scientists as Stephen Hawking, Carlos Frenk, and Michael Turner,[1] most scientists are still unaware of them. Though major newspapers and prime-time television have covered much of the news about them, the public is still largely in the dark.

But for the first time ever, the explosion of knowledge provides enough information to understand scientific ideas written down over 2000 years ago—insights that only the Creator of the universe could have known.

Scientists Speak Out[2]

"I find more sure marks of authenticity in the Bible than in any profane history whatsoever."

Sir Isaac Newton
—developed the laws of motion, calculus

"With regard to the origin of life, science . . . positively affirms creative power."

Lord Kelvin
—established thermodynamics as a science

"[It is] as difficult to understand a scientist who does not acknowledge the presence [of God] . . . as it is to comprehend a theologian who would deny the advances of science."

Wernher von Braun
—space scientist, past director of NASA

The Key Issues

The Bible has been analyzed *far* more than any
work in the history of the world.

Is there a God? Does He interact with the world and with human
beings? Does He communicate with us? If so, how? Why should
we presume the Bible somehow stands apart from other writings
that claim to be "inspired"?

Common Questions

Does God exist?
No — Then explain: Creation Life
Yes — Who is He, She, or It?

Does God interact with people?
No — Then explain: Historical miracles
Yes — How?

Does God communicate with people?
No — Then explain: The miraculous information in the Bible
Yes — How? / What is the message?

Proposed Sources for Answers

Astrology
Psychics
Numerology
Ouija Board
Tarot Cards
Vinaya Pitaka
Abidhamma Pitaka
Sutta Pitaka
The Vedas
The Upanishads
Ramayana
Mahabharata
Bhagavad Gita
The Puranas
The Five Classics
The Tao Te King
Ko-ji-ki
Nihongi
Avesta
Qur'an
Granth Sahib
The Humanist Manifesto
The Book of Mormon
Doctrine and Covenants
Pearl of Great Price
The Divine Principle
Science and Health
The Watchtower

The Bible

Tests of Communication from God

1. There should be *no mistakes* in the original inspired writing.

2. There should be undeniable evidence the communication was from God (for example, fulfilled prophecy or scientific foresight).

In these two tests, the Bible stands alone—confirmed over centuries by many thousands of scholars.

The scientific insights within the Bible show:

(1) *accuracy,* and

(2) *inspiration from God*

—because the insights were recorded correctly long before they were discovered by human beings.

How the Bible Fits with History

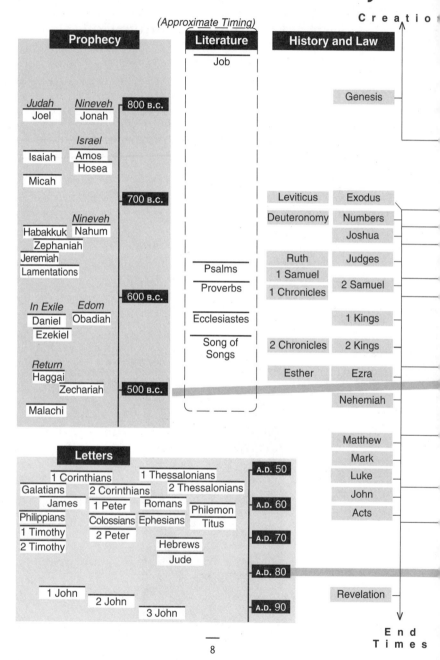

(Approximate Timing)

C r e a t i o

Prophecy	Literature	History and Law

Literature

Job

History and Law

Genesis

Judah — 800 B.C. — *Nineveh*
Joel — Jonah

Israel
Isaiah — Amos
Hosea
Micah

— 700 B.C. —

Nineveh
Habakkuk — Nahum
Zephaniah
Jeremiah
Lamentations

Leviticus — Exodus
Deuteronomy — Numbers
Joshua

Ruth — Judges
Psalms
1 Samuel
Proverbs — 2 Samuel
1 Chronicles

In Exile *Edom* — 600 B.C. —
Daniel — Obadiah
Ezekiel

Ecclesiastes — 1 Kings

Song of
Songs — 2 Chronicles — 2 Kings

Return
Haggai
Zechariah — 500 B.C. —
Esther — Ezra

Malachi — Nehemiah

Matthew

Letters

Mark

1 Corinthians — 1 Thessalonians — A.D. 50 — Luke
Galatians — 2 Corinthians — 2 Thessalonians
James — 1 Peter — Romans — John
Philippians — Colossians — Ephesians — Philemon — A.D. 60 — Acts
1 Timothy — 2 Peter — Titus
2 Timothy

Hebrews — A.D. 70
Jude

1 John — A.D. 80

2 John — Revelation

3 John — A.D. 90

E n d
T i m e s

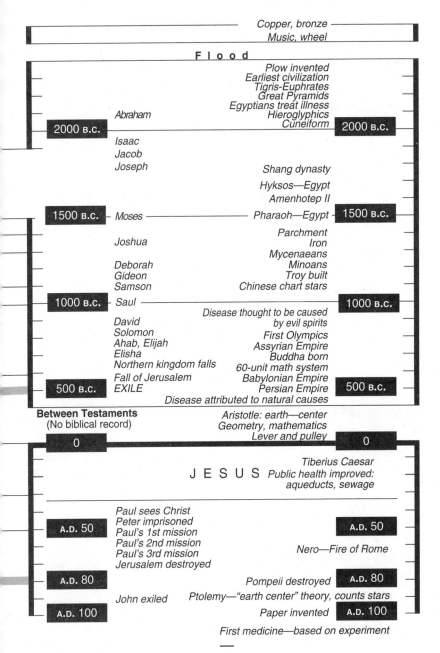

Copper, bronze
Music, wheel

F l o o d

Plow invented
Earliest civilization
Tigris-Euphrates
Great Pyramids
Egyptians treat illness
Abraham   Hieroglyphics
Cuneiform

2000 B.C. | **2000 B.C.**

Isaac
Jacob
Joseph   Shang dynasty

Hyksos—Egypt
Amenhotep II

1500 B.C. Moses ———— Pharaoh—Egypt **1500 B.C.**

Parchment
Joshua   Iron
Mycenaeans
Deborah   Minoans
Gideon   Troy built
Samson   Chinese chart stars

1000 B.C. Saul ——————— **1000 B.C.**
Disease thought to be caused
David   by evil spirits
Solomon   First Olympics
Ahab, Elijah   Assyrian Empire
Elisha   Buddha born
Northern kingdom falls 60-unit math system
Fall of Jerusalem   Babylonian Empire
500 B.C. EXILE   Persian Empire **500 B.C.**
Disease attributed to natural causes

Between Testaments   Aristotle: earth—center
(No biblical record)   Geometry, mathematics
0   Lever and pulley **0**

Tiberius Caesar
J E S U S Public health improved:
aqueducts, sewage

Paul sees Christ
Peter imprisoned
A.D. 50 Paul's 1st mission **A.D. 50**
Paul's 2nd mission
Paul's 3rd mission   Nero—Fire of Rome
Jerusalem destroyed

A.D. 80   Pompeii destroyed **A.D. 80**

John exiled   Ptolemy—"earth center" theory, counts stars
A.D. 100   Paper invented **A.D. 100**

First medicine—based on experiment

9

An Overview of the Bible Relative to Science

The Bible accurately recorded many ideas long before science understood them. In fact, human thinking was often opposite to what was later found to be correct.

The Book of Genesis

Genesis begins with a summary of how God created the heavens and earth. Thousands of years later, science has confirmed that the account in Genesis of events of creation matches the actual way the world was formed.[7,8] Genesis also reviews God's judgment of the world with the great flood—an event confirmed by the traditional accounts of virtually every culture in the world. Scientific research also offers strong evidence of the flood.[3,4,5]

Not surprisingly, archaeology has defined the "cradle of civilization" to be the Tigris-Euphrates valley. This lush valley was the richest, most habitable terrain just south of the mountains of Ararat—the resting place of Noah's ark. Archaeological evidence

of early Genesis events in the region includes "tower of Babel" structures (Genesis 11) and very early metalworking and musical implements (Genesis 4:21,22). Genesis also describes the selection of Abraham to become father of a nation that would be . . .

... used to communicate God's
message to the world.

Among many other things, God told Abraham to move hundreds of miles to a new, promised land in Canaan from his hometown of Ur, which was in the Tigris-Euphrates region. Bronze, the wheel, and writing existed in this area, as well as the major invention of the plow.

Genesis relates how Abraham and Sarah gave birth to a miracle child, Isaac, who became the father of Jacob, father to the 12 future leaders of the tribes of Israel. Egypt was a prominent power at the time, and the Great Pyramids were well under way. Genesis ends with the account of how Jacob's son Joseph, sold as a slave by his brothers, became a powerful leader in Egypt and saved his family from famine. The entire family of Jacob moved to Egypt (where the Hebrew descendants eventually became slaves). Much of Genesis is a foreshadowing of the coming Messiah, and it contains many prophecies of the birth, sacrifice, and role of Jesus.

Science in the era of Genesis was confined to basic mathematics and some charting of the heavens. Despite amazing building projects, there was little understanding of physics. Although the Egyptians systematically treated disease, the cause of disease was thought to be evil spirits. The natural cause of disease was not discovered until about 400 B.C.—and the role of germs was not known until the 1800s.

The Other Books of Moses

The next four books, Exodus, Leviticus, Numbers, and Deuteronomy, complete the five books of the *Torah* (the books of law) written by Moses about 1500 B.C. These books contain several laws that protected the Hebrews from diseases afflicting the Egyptians (Exodus 15:26)—giving medical information not understood until the nineteenth century. The books expand these important matters:

1. God's delivery of His people by dramatic, miraculous events using ordinary people (the book of Exodus).

2. God's law defined (the books of Leviticus and Deuteronomy).

3. God's judgment exemplified (the books of Exodus and Numbers).

4. God's prophecy of the Savior to come (all books).

Moses led the Israelites out of slavery in Egypt—their deliverance highlighted by God's miraculous parting of the Red Sea. The next 40 years of wandering in the wilderness was an important time for God to reveal His nature through the experiences of the nation as it learned about Him. The Bible makes this period of teaching available to all mankind. Although the nation was being directed by God (a theocracy), the Hebrew people had free will and often chose to disobey God—as the consequences showed.

The Promised Land

(1400 B.C.–1050 B.C.)

Joshua led the Israelites into Canaan, the land God had promised Abraham centuries before. At first, the Hebrew people had dramatic victories everywhere—victories that clearly demonstrated God's power through perfectly fulfilled prophecy. Archaeology has confirmed many events to have occurred precisely as indicated in the Bible.

The books of Judges and Ruth continue to elaborate on the early settlement of the land of Canaan. The time of Judges was one of increasing disobedience by Israel and was marred by problems with neighboring enemies and within the tribes of Israel itself. The events of Ruth took place in the hills of Bethlehem. At a time of national disobedience, Ruth (a Gentile) obeyed God and was given a husband. Ruth became King David's great-grandmother and an ancestor of Jesus Christ.

The Time of the Kings

(1050 B.C.–400 B.C.)

The historical books of Samuel (two books), Chronicles (two books), and Kings (two books) describe the evolving Jewish nation during the time it was ruled by kings. Although God intended Himself to be the leader of the Jewish nation, the desire of the people to have a king was eventually granted by God. The kingdom of Israel was unified starting in 1050 B.C. under three successive kings: Saul, David, and Solomon (each reigned 40 years). After Solomon, the kingdom became divided in 930 B.C. Both Israel (the northern kingdom) and Judah (the southern kingdom) increasingly fell into apostasy. Israel was conquered by the Assyrians in 722 B.C., and Judah was exiled to Babylon starting in 606 B.C. (the exile was complete in 587 B.C.).

Science in the period of the kings was not much more advanced than in the time of Abraham. People still had little understanding of microscopic issues (for example, germs) or telescopic issues (the heavens, for example). From a biblical perspective, however, the period of the kings is an especially important time for God's communication to mankind through the Bible because:

1. *It provides many real-life examples of the interaction of people with God.* David was considered "a man after God's own heart." He was often in God's favor and gave heartfelt praise and worship to God, as recorded in many of the Psalms. Yet David was also an adulterer and a murderer—and suffered consequences for his actions as all humans do. Despite all this, David was revered by Israel and was a key ancestor of Jesus Christ. Many other examples, both good and bad, come from the lives of people in this period.

2. *It provides breadth of understanding of God.* Most Psalms (songs) and other "poetry-style" books (Ecclesiastes, Proverbs, and Song of Songs) were created during this period. They provide insight into different ways to understand God. The Psalms also contain several concepts about astronomy, geology, and physics that were not discovered until recent centuries. Job, a unique book of literature that was written hundreds of years prior to the period, gives us particularly significant insight into suffering and evil. Job contains many surprising scientific insights (see pages 24,25).

3. *It was the setting for books written specifically by "the prophets."*
Seventeen books of prophecy were written during this period.
Of the 300-plus prophecies contained in these books, many
were immediately fulfilled. Others foretold in incredible detail
the Savior who was to come (Jesus Christ). Several of the prophetic books contain important scientific insights.

The other Old Testament books of Ezra, Esther, and Nehemiah
contain important facts of history that provide a complete picture
of the historical scope and the prophecy of the Bible. Ezra and
Nehemiah deal with the return of Israel from exile, describing
events which demonstrate the precise fulfillment of prophecy.
Esther shows God's care for Jews who did not return from exile.

Old Testament Summary

The Old Testament provides an in-depth view of the *nature of God,*
the *nature of mankind,* and a history of the *relationship of mankind
and God.* It clarifies that mankind needs a Savior.

Just as important, the Old Testament contains both a *specific
prophetic message of a Savior* who was to come—along with a
concealed message that verifies that the information is in fact from
God (thus providing future generations assurance of its reliability).

Between the Testaments

(400 B.C.–A.D. 50)

The world was still largely ignorant. The earth was considered the
center of the universe. During this time disease was first attributed
to natural causes, not evil spirits.

The Gospels

The Gospels of Matthew, Mark, Luke, and John describe the life of Jesus on earth from four different perspectives. Matthew, a tax collector, wrote to show that Jesus was the promised Messiah and the "King." Mark described Jesus as the suffering servant who became the ultimate sacrifice for mankind. Luke, a physician, emphasized the human side of Jesus. And John focused on His deity.

All four Gospels reveal the nature of Jesus through His teaching, His miracles, and the detailed account of His death and resurrection. All four Gospels also reveal the detail-by-detail fulfillment of Old Testament prophecy in Jesus. The book of Acts, also written by Luke, reveals Jesus' impact after His resurrection. It describes the fulfillment of more prophecies, including the appearance of Jesus in Galilee, the arrival of the Holy Spirit at Pentecost, the empowering of the disciples to perform miracles in Jesus' name, and the rapid expansion of the church.

There are several references in the New Testament that touch on science, mostly dealing with the advanced laws of physics discovered in the twentieth century. Meanwhile, civilization was gradually advancing. Rome was beginning to use plumbing (not because the need for sanitation was understood, but for the sake of convenience and cleanliness).

The Letters

Apart from the Gospels, the remainder of the New Testament consists mostly of letters clarifying and expanding on the role and teaching of Jesus. Paul, an avid enemy and murderer of Christians, converted immediately to Christianity upon seeing the risen Christ.

He is responsible for at least 13 of the letters (books) of the New Testament. Thessalonians (two books) focuses on the second coming of Jesus. Corinthians (two books), Galatians, Romans, Philippians, Colossians, and Ephesians all deal with problems of the new churches and believers. They explain the doctrine taught by Jesus and provide guidance for conduct of Christians and church leaders. Paul's individual letters to Timothy (two books), Titus, and Philemon all had specific purposes. The letters to Timothy encouraged him and directed him in the path of becoming a good church leader. The letter to Titus instructed him in the selection of church leaders and defined Christian behavior. The letter to Philemon requested assistance for a runaway slave (Onesimus) and exemplifies the change Jesus Christ can make in a person.

The letter to the Hebrews (writer unknown) defines the prominence of Jesus. His greatness is placed higher than the greatness of Moses, Joshua, all the prophets, all the high priests, and even the angels. This placed Him in perspective for the Jews. James and Jude, written by the natural (half) brothers of Jesus (who became disciples *after* the resurrection) instruct believers how to live their lives. Jude defines the consequences for anyone guilty of false teaching and asks people to defend the true teaching of Jesus. Peter's two and John's three letters are instructional messages for believers.

The final book of the Bible, Revelation, was written by John in exile at the end of his life. It contains the detailed revelation that Jesus gave to John regarding the end of time. Revelation is written in a cryptic, symbolic style.

Why Science Seems
at Odds
with the Bible

The more the Bible is studied, the more surprising it becomes
that people often *think* it is in conflict with science. Yet science's
rejection of the Bible has become common only in the last
hundred years. Great scientists of the past, including Newton,
Kepler, and Galileo, were all avid readers and believers of the
Bible. As scientists are slowly becoming aware of the incredible
wealth of recently discovered information, a scientific return to
the Bible is occurring.

The decline in a scientific belief in God can be traced to Darwin's
theory of evolution, introduced in 1860. This alternative to creation, combined with the prevalent theory of an infinite universe, caused many scientists to turn away from God and the
Bible. But even as early as 1916, Einstein's general relativity
breakthrough contained ample evidence to refute evolution with
pure mathematical probability (reviewed in *Creation vs. Evolution*
in the *Examine the Evidence* series). Only in recent years has general relativity been essentially "proven" (Einstein begrudgingly
admitted the probability of a Creator[8]). Unfortunately, the world
is slow to recognize the new scientific evidence supporting the
Bible—and much outdated information is still in the textbooks of
students. Scientific evidence of God is now increasing *extremely
rapidly*—and gradually the scientific world is becoming aware of
the many new breakthroughs.

A Probabilistic View of the Bible

Anyone knowledgeable in probability theory and also
knowledgeable about the Bible should understand the
supernatural inspiration of the Bible. Consider these points:

1. The information in the Bible could not have been contrived after scientific knowledge became available. The Dead Sea scrolls and the Septuagint—both written hundreds of years before Christ—exist as evidence.

2. The books of the Bible were written by at least 40 authors over 1500 years, yet they have consistent integrated information that ties them all together.

The Bible is simply statistically impossible *without divine inspiration.* Consider these points also:

*   *Scientific insights* are in the Bible that were not uncovered by science until many centuries later (see pages 24,25). Beliefs at the time of the recording of these insights contradicted them. The probability of such insights— without God—is so small as to be beyond reason.

*   *Prophecy miracles* predict details of the future (see *Does the Bible Predict the Future?* in the *Examine the Evidence* series). The chance of the prophecies about Jesus alone coming true, after having been written centuries in advance, vastly exceeds the point of statistical absurdity—without the inspiration of God.

*   *Concealed codes* reveal incredibly complex models and patterns in the Bible that integrate books by different authors from different locations and from different times (see *Are There Hidden Codes in the Bible?* in the *Examine the Evidence* series).

*   *Creation.* Even if Moses had somehow known the ten-event creation process (see pages 22,23), merely *guessing* the correct order would be *highly unlikely* (one chance in about 4 million*). Recent discoveries show that life and the existence of the earth are statistically impossible without God.

---

* This is about the same as one's chance of winning a lottery with the purchase of one ticket. We are far more likely to be struck by lightning.

Evidence for Creation
Life on Earth

Creation itself is strong evidence supporting the existence of God and the biblical account (see *Creation vs. Evolution* in the *Examine the Evidence* series). Following is a partial summary of some of the scientific evidence of creation, which ties in directly to the Genesis record (see pages 22,23).

The Uniqueness of Planet Earth

The justification for the search for other planets like earth seems far-fetched to astrophysicists who have studied the extreme "fine tuning" necessary to make earth suitable for habitation. Consider just the events of the first "two days" of the Genesis creation event alone (the creation of the proper atmosphere and the establishment of the hydrologic cycle). The probability of the combination of the factors necessary to achieve just these two criteria for life to exist is estimated to be one in a hundred trillion trillion (one in 10^{26}). With a *maximum* total number of planets of perhaps 10^{22} (an estimate considered generous), the chance of another life-supporting planet is extremely remote. If we add to this the probability of the occurrence of the other factors needed for life, the chance of life on another planet becomes *absurdly small*.

The delicate balance in the design of the earth is illustrated by the following examples from a list of over forty criteria determined to be critical for life on earth.

Life could *not* exist on earth if *any one* of the following were the case:

- *slower rotation of the earth*
- *faster rotation of the earth*
- *the earth 2–5% farther from the sun*
- *the earth 2–5% closer to the sun*
- *1% change in sunlight reaching the earth*
- *a smaller earth*
- *a larger earth*
- *a smaller moon*
- *a larger moon*
- *more than one moon*
- *the earth's crust thinner*
- *the earth's crust thicker*
- *oxygen/nitrogen ratio greater*
- *oxygen/nitrogen ratio less*
- *more or less ozone*

The Amazing "Timed Collision"[6]

Scientists are fairly certain that a heavenly body about half the size of Mars collided with the earth at precisely the right time in the earth's development (evidence exists that confirms this). The collision "knocked" much of the carbon dioxide (CO_2) out of the earth's atmosphere, averting a life-preventing "runaway greenhouse effect" and allowing the right atmospheric chemistry. It also increased the speed of the earth's rotation (an important factor). The moon was formed from part of the colliding body, and it became a vital element in stabilizing the earth's axis and rotation, thus creating the environment for life. The odds of this event happening in such a precise way *without God* are small *beyond reason.*

How Much Proof . . . Is Really *Proof?*

If someone told you he or she could pick the winning lottery number, then *did*—you might be impressed. The odds of this are, maybe, one in ten million (or 1 in 10^7). Does this "prove" the person has divine knowledge? Maybe and maybe not—though it is *very, very* impressive. Now suppose this person did it twice in a row (one chance in a hundred thousand billion—10^{14}). It would suddenly seem obvious this individual had "special" information.

From a practical standpoint, scientists have determined that anything whose probability is less than one chance in 10^{50} is beyond reason—essentially impossible or absurd (like someone correctly picking the lottery seven times in a row)—*unless* there is "special" knowledge involved. Odds *far* more staggering than this describe the presence of God's "fingerprints" in the Bible.

The Creation Events of Genesis 1

Thorough understanding of Genesis 1 requires considering the *original Hebrew text*. The English translation can be misleading. For example, in regard to day four, verse 16 might imply that the sun and moon were created after the formation of plants—a problem for scientists. The actual Hebrew verb and tense used, when taken together with the words in 1:1, correctly indicate that the sun and moon *"became visible"* at the surface of the earth on day four (but all heavenly bodies were *previously* created).

Reviewing the order of events of creation shows the Bible is accurate as far as science can verify. It's important to notice the *vantage point* (frame of reference) of "God's spirit"—hovering over the waters (verse 2).

The Events of Creation As Confirmed by Science[7,8]

1. **The heavenly bodies created** (Genesis 1:1)—The earth was initially covered with a thick layer of gas and dust *that did not allow light to penetrate*. This is probably a standard initial condition of planets of the earth's mass and temperature. The initial conditions of the earth described in the Bible are accepted by science: dark, formless, and void.

2. **"Let there be light"** (1:3)—The atmosphere became translucent to allow *some* light to reach the surface of the water, a critical prerequisite for the introduction of life (light allows photosynthesis).

3. **The development of the hydrologic cycle** (1:6,7)—The "perfect" conditions of temperature, pressure, and distance from the sun allow the existence of all forms of H_2O (solid, liquid, and vapor)—all necessary for life.

4. **The formation of land and sea** (1:9,10)—Seismic and volcanic activity occurred in the precise degree to allow 30 percent of the earth's surface to become and remain land. Scientists have determined this is the ideal ratio to promote the greatest complexity of life-forms.

5. **The creation of vegetation** (1:11)—Light, water, and large amounts of carbon dioxide set the stage for vegetation. This was the first life-form.

6. **Atmospheric transparency** (1:14,15)—Plants gradually produced oxygen to a level of 21 percent of the atmosphere. This (and other factors) caused a transparent atmosphere to form and permitted "lights in the heavens" to become visible at the surface of the earth, marking day and night and seasons.

7. **The creation of small sea animals and birds** (1:20,21)—Scientists agree these were the first animal life-forms of all classes discussed in the Bible.

8. **The creation of land animals** (1:24,25)—The final life-forms prior to human beings were created: quadrupeds and rodents.

9. **The creation of human beings** (1:26,27)—The final creature made its appearance on earth.

10. **No additional creation** (Genesis 2:2)—No unique creation has occurred since.

Historical Comparison . . .

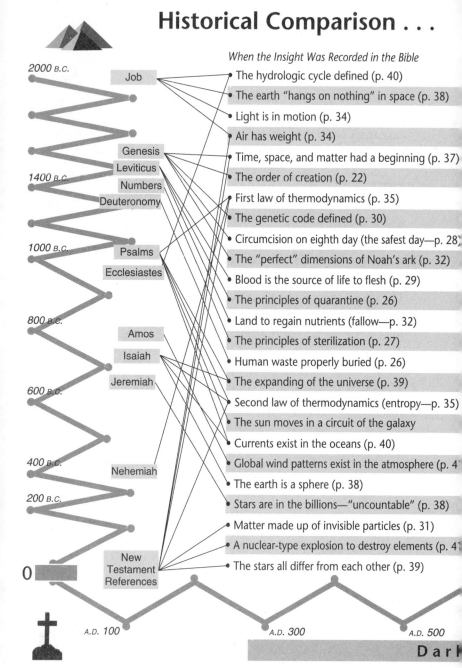

When the Insight Was Recorded in the Bible

2000 B.C.

Job — The hydrologic cycle defined (p. 40)

The earth "hangs on nothing" in space (p. 38)

Light is in motion (p. 34)

Air has weight (p. 34)

Genesis — Time, space, and matter had a beginning (p. 37)

Leviticus

1400 B.C. — The order of creation (p. 22)

Numbers — First law of thermodynamics (p. 35)

Deuteronomy — The genetic code defined (p. 30)

Circumcision on eighth day (the safest day—p. 28)

1000 B.C.

Psalms — The "perfect" dimensions of Noah's ark (p. 32)

Ecclesiastes — Blood is the source of life to flesh (p. 29)

The principles of quarantine (p. 26)

Land to regain nutrients (fallow—p. 32)

800 B.C.

Amos — The principles of sterilization (p. 27)

Isaiah — Human waste properly buried (p. 26)

Jeremiah — The expanding of the universe (p. 39)

600 B.C. — Second law of thermodynamics (entropy—p. 35)

The sun moves in a circuit of the galaxy

Currents exist in the oceans (p. 40)

400 B.C.

Nehemiah — Global wind patterns exist in the atmosphere (p. 4?)

The earth is a sphere (p. 38)

200 B.C. — Stars are in the billions—"uncountable" (p. 38)

Matter made up of invisible particles (p. 31)

A nuclear-type explosion to destroy elements (p. 4?)

New
Testament — The stars all differ from each other (p. 39)
References

0

A.D. 100   A.D. 300   A.D. 500

D a r k

. . . of Scientific Insights

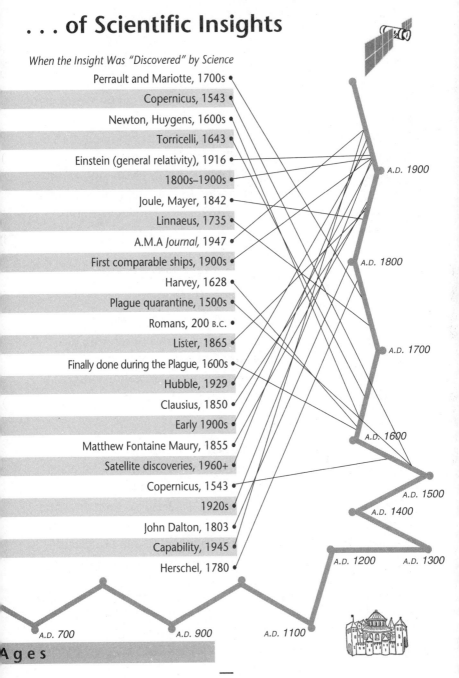

When the Insight Was "Discovered" by Science

Perrault and Mariotte, 1700s
Copernicus, 1543
Newton, Huygens, 1600s
Torricelli, 1643
Einstein (general relativity), 1916
1800s–1900s
Joule, Mayer, 1842
Linnaeus, 1735
A.M.A *Journal*, 1947
First comparable ships, 1900s
Harvey, 1628
Plague quarantine, 1500s
Romans, 200 B.C.
Lister, 1865
Finally done during the Plague, 1600s
Hubble, 1929
Clausius, 1850
Early 1900s
Matthew Fontaine Maury, 1855
Satellite discoveries, 1960+
Copernicus, 1543
1920s
John Dalton, 1803
Capability, 1945
Herschel, 1780

A.D. 1900
A.D. 1800
A.D. 1700
A.D. 1600
A.D. 1500
A.D. 1400
A.D. 1300
A.D. 1200
A.D. 1100
A.D. 900
A.D. 700

A ges

25

Insights into Medicine

It's surprising that some of the most obvious medical practices today—though outlined in the Bible—were not "discovered" until recently. In about 1500 B.C., the Hebrews, led by Moses, left Egypt and faced the rugged challenge of surviving away from a well-developed civilization. Aside from merely surviving, they needed to become strong enough to conquer a new land. God promised that by following His laws, the Hebrews would avoid the diseases of the Egyptians (Exodus 15:26). The Bible's ancient laws have tremendous medical insights not known until the germ research of the late 1800s.

Principles of Quarantine and Waste Disposal

When the Black Plague was killing much of Europe prior to the Renaissance, desperate nations turned to the church for guidance. Returning to the Old Testament laws of Moses, they instituted principles practiced by the Israelites for dealing with diseases like leprosy, for handling of the dead, and for waste disposal.

Quarantine is well understood today as a control of infectious disease. In the days of Moses and in the days of the Black Plague, however, God's command (Leviticus 13) had to be obeyed without people knowing why. Leviticus 13:45,46 commands the sick to let others know of their illness in an obvious (and bizarre) way—while covering their mouths they had to yell "Unclean! Unclean!" They also had to remain outside the camp until cured.

Poor waste disposal practices led to the spread of the Black Death (the Plague). The Bible provided insight regarding the burying of human waste (Deuteronomy 23:12-14). Even the method of handling the dead was outlined in the Bible (Numbers 19). Desperation caused a return to biblical laws in the 1600s, and the dreaded Plague was finally controlled.

Sterilization

Another biblical insight not understood until the late 1800s is the principle of basic sterilization (washing of hands and clothing). Guidelines for washing are stressed in the handling of the dead (Numbers 19). Basic purification practices (some ceremonial) and methods to control contamination are also specified for many other cases including: "unclean" food (Leviticus 11:29-40), childbirth (Leviticus 12), bodily discharges (Leviticus 15), and infection (Leviticus 13). Even with ceremonial sacrifice and offerings, protection from disease was ensured by thorough burning and washing (for example Leviticus 6:8-13).

In the 1840s the poignant tragedy of nonscientific, nonbiblical medical practices was demonstrated by a Viennese doctor, Ignaz Semmelweis. In his obstetrics ward he noticed an unusually high death rate for women examined by teachers and students. The daily practice was to perform autopsies on the dead in the morning and later (without washing) give pelvic exams to new patients. A new practice of thorough washing after autopsies was instituted by the doctor. But it was greeted by sharp ridicule and disdain from his colleagues. Although deaths dropped sharply, Semmelweis's contract was not renewed. Upon his leaving, washing stopped, and deaths again sharply increased. Semmelweis, despondent, eventually died in a mental institution. The guidelines within the Bible were not recognized until 1865 by Joseph Lister, an honored scientist and a Christian.[9]

Circumcision

No one really knows for sure why God specifically chose the rite of circumcision as the sign of His covenant with Abraham (Genesis 17:11). Though it seems like an odd practice, scholars have viewed it as a symbolic "blood" sacrifice that shows an irrevocable commitment to God (similar to a marriage vow). Perhaps the reproductive system was involved to remind people that God is the ultimate creator of life—or that people's ability to create life is a gift from God.

Circumcision has been shown to have medical value. Research in the mid-1900s found that Jewish women had a remarkably low rate of cervical cancer. Further study identified the major cause of cervical cancer to be the smegma bacillus, which can easily be carried in the foreskin of uncircumcised males and transmitted to women having abrasions of the cervix (such as occur in childbirth).[9]

God also commanded that male Jews be circumcised on the eighth day after birth (Genesis 17:12). Why the eighth day? Research[9] shows that newborn infants are particularly susceptible to hemorrhaging from the second day after birth to the fifth. A small cut can be deadly. Vitamin K, necessary for the production of prothrombin (the body's blood-clotting substance) is not present sufficiently until days five

Venereal Disease

The Bible tells of a man, blind from birth, who was healed by Jesus. The disciples asked "who sinned, the blind man or his parents?" (John 9:1-7). We now know venereal disease is the leading cause of blindness in infants. In countries where silver nitrate is not applied to the eyes of newborns, many of them become blind. Parental sin can cause blindness.

through seven. The prothrombin level is only 30 percent of normal on day three but skyrockets to 110 percent of normal on the eighth day before it levels off. God's command to circumcise on day eight turns out to be the safest practice.

Blood As a Life Source to the Flesh

Only comparatively recently has medicine recognized that blood is in fact the life source to all parts of the body. It provides oxygen and carries vital nutrients that are essential for life. The Bible indicated this fact 1500 years before Christ (Leviticus 17:11)—"the life of the flesh is in its blood." For centuries, physicians would drain blood from patients in an attempt to rid the body of poison, which resulted in death for many people (and possibly contributed to George Washington's).

Stress—and Moderation—in Daily Living

The Bible is filled with practical advice and commands about things we now take for granted. Some examples include warnings against abuse of alcohol, warnings against gluttony, and warnings against sexual immorality.

Some of the most insightful teaching of the Bible is about stress, now widely regarded as a major health threat. In many places the Bible emphasizes the need for forgiveness and love and warns against things like resentment and anger. Medical insights from the Bible are now seen to extend into all areas of health: physical, mental, and emotional.

Insights into Biology and Chemistry

The Bible clearly indicates that God is revealed through His creation (see the insert below). Recent breakthroughs in molecular biology emphasize God's handiwork. However, on a far more basic level the Bible accurately refers to aspects of biology and chemistry long before man understood these sciences.

Genetic Classification

It surprises most people to learn that science had little understanding of even basic species classification until 1735, when the Swede Carolus Linnaeus developed an organism classification system—still used in part today. The Bible defined biological classification by reproducing "kind" (Genesis 1:21-31).

The Bible Says to See God in Nature

The Bible repeatedly tells us to see and marvel at God through the world around us:

Job 10:8-14	Psalm 19:1-6	Proverbs 8:22-33
Job 12:7-10	Psalm 50:6	Ecclesiastes 3:11
Job 34:14,15	Psalm 85:11	Habakkuk 3:3
Job 35:5-7	Psalm 97:6	Acts 14:17
Job 37:5-7	Psalm 98:2,3	Acts 17:23
Job 38–41	Psalm 104	Romans 1:18-25
Colossians 1:23	Psalm 139	Romans 2:14,15

Moreover, the concept of "same kind" reproducing species was properly described when Noah was commanded to bring each "kind" of life into the ark to preserve them for a future "new beginning" of life on earth (Genesis 7:1-16). (Ironically, although we now know that a totally new species cannot be created by cross-species breeding—evolutionary theory implies otherwise.)

Another example of a biblical insight into genetics is in a letter by Paul to the church of Corinth (1 Corinthians 15:38,39). Paul refers to the differences between each class of organism in regard to both plants and animals. Interestingly, he uses this illustration to indicate the type of heavenly bodies humans can expect to have, which are differentiated from all other forms of organisms—thus further distinguishing humans from animals.

Atoms and Molecules

In 400 B.C. the Greek philosopher Democritus speculated that matter was made of tiny, invisible particles, which he called atoms. His idea was regarded with skepticism. The great scientists of the time, including Aristotle, thought that all matter was made up of various proportions of earth, air, fire, and water. The Bible correctly described matter as being created from "things unseen" (Hebrews 11:3). Science finally caught up in 1803, when John Dalton developed the modern atomic theory.

What Is a Living Organism?

The design of a single living cell is far more complex than the most advanced computer or airplane. Not only are living organisms capable of more functions, faster, and in a smaller space, but living things have abilities far beyond the most complex machines (for example, creative thought, reproduction, self-diagnosis, and healing). The genius of human inventors is widely recognized, yet some reject the far greater genius of the Creator of life.

Insights into Engineering and Agriculture

One would not expect the Bible to contain specific information about the applied sciences. Yet, in addition to its medical insights, it has a few surprising insights into engineering and agriculture that were not discovered until hundreds of years later.

Engineering

The ark of Noah—The detailed design of the ark of Noah is an example of an engineering design far ahead of its time. Naval engineers now know that the length-to-width ratio specified in the Bible (Genesis 6:15) is ideal for the stability of a barge-type craft (a non-propelled ship) designed for rough seas.[1] It was not until the 1900s that comparably sized ships were constructed. Other details of construction, including the waterproofing, roof and deck structure, and the design of the opening for light (18" near the roof) all display sound engineering.

Apart from the dimensions of the ark, its material was an important factor in providing adequate strength. The Bible defines the wood as "gopher wood" which scholars believe is either an ancient form of plywood or an exotic wood of that region. In either case, the wood had to be considerably stronger than oak. In the past, the largest vessels safely constructed with oak for heavy seas have been limited to about 350 feet in length. However, some exotic woods approach the strength of steel.

Buildings—Although several buildings and structures are mentioned in the Bible, only the temple (1 Kings 6; 2 Chronicles 2–4) and tabernacle (Exodus 25–27) were based on designs directed by God. The engineering of both buildings is basic, simple, and effective. Of greater significance is the architecture, which skillfully integrates complex symbology and purpose with good design. The artistic significance and beauty of these structures, admired for centuries, are often viewed as designs that were ahead of their time.

In addition to scientific insights, the Bible provides an accurate historical account of the technical knowledge of the period. "Tower of Babel" structures complete with "baked bricks" (Genesis 11) have been found in Mesopotamia. And many building design features, ranging from the doors of Lot's house (Genesis 19:9) to the columns of Solomon's palace (1 Kings 7), have been confirmed by archaeology.

Agricultural Insights

Agriculture was of extreme importance to ancient man. Hence advances in agriculture preceded knowledge in other disciplines. For example, the plow (an extremely important invention) first appeared in about 3000 B.C. in the areas of Mesopotamia and Egypt.

God added an important insight to the Bible by commanding the Israelites to "give the land a rest every seventh year" (Leviticus 25:4). Today, the need to replenish soil with nutrients by crop rotation and the principle of "fallow" (resting the land) is well known. Although the command in Leviticus was written about 1500 B.C., the first evidence of the practice (other than in Israel) was its application by the Romans about 200 B.C. And it's conceivable Rome learned of the practice from Israel.

Insights into Physics

The facts and laws of physics that we take for granted today were generally not discovered until the last few hundred years. Yet even when the scientific world thought certain facts were in conflict with the Bible, many great minds of science accepted the word of the Bible as true based on faith alone. Today, we have the knowledge and evidence to support the faith of earlier great scientists.

Air Has Weight

From the days of Aristotle through the Dark Ages and Renaissance and until fairly recently, the scientific world believed that air was weightless. The Bible indicates otherwise. The ancient book of Job, written as early as 2000 B.C., indicates that air has "weight" (Job 28:25—see King James or NASB translations). Science, however, didn't acknowledge the weight of air until the discovery of barometric pressure by Torricelli, an Italian, in 1643.

Light Moves

People once thought light was instantaneous. After all, the tremendous velocity of light certainly made it seem to appear instantaneously. Not only do we now know that light moves, but that its movement and velocity is critical to our very existence. The velocity of light has now been measured many times. Newton and Huygens first confirmed the motion of light in the 1600s. Yet nearly 4000 years prior to that, the book of Job implied that light moves from one place to another (Job 38:19,20).

The First Law of Thermodynamics

No knowledgeable scientist disputes the first law of thermodynamics, which states that energy cannot be created or destroyed. This was discovered independently by two scientists, Joule and Mayer, in the same year—1842. The Bible, however, makes reference to the idea that no mass or energy has been input into the universe since God finished the creation process. Genesis (2:2,3) and Hebrews (4:3,4) speak of God having "finished" creation. (Other references to "completion" include Psalm 148:6; Isaiah 40:26; 2 Peter 3:3-7; and Hebrews 4:10).

The Second Law of Thermodynamics

The second law of thermodynamics, the law of entropy, was defined in 1850 by Clausius. Entropy, in its simplest sense, means that things tend to move from a state of order to disorder (randomness). In other words, things tend to decay over time. Stars burn out. Springs unwind. Heat dissipates. Materials become mixed and co-mingled. Only when energy is purposefully added can order be gained out of a state of deterioration. (Among many other things, this is an argument against evolution, since increasing the complexity of species without the purposeful input of a Creator would violate the law of entropy.) As with the first law, the Bible has many direct or indirect references to entropy (Psalm 102:25,26; Isaiah 51:6; Matthew 24:35; Romans 8:20-22; 1 John 2:17; Hebrews 12:27).

Insights into Physics
Twentieth Century Discoveries

Perhaps the most complex and rapidly advancing area of science is physics. One might think the Bible would contain many inconsistencies with modern physics, considering that many of the most significant discoveries didn't occur until the twentieth century. Ironically, it has taken the recent breakthroughs in science to help people realize that the Bible is accurate.

Time Had a Beginning

General relativity is a subject the average individual would choose to ignore. Most people view it as a lot of mathematics—just a theory of Dr. Albert Einstein. The truth is, it's much more. When Einstein was alive, general relativity could be proven only to a 90 percent level of certainty. Even so, it caused Einstein to switch from complete atheism to belief in some kind of Creator. Today, general relativity has been proven to the certainty of 10^{26+++}. It is essentially fact. So what does it mean?

The essence (without the equations) is that matter, gravity, time, energy, and acceleration are all

Sir Isaac Newton— A Defender of the Bible[2]

It's ironic that Isaac Newton, discoverer of the laws of motion that were later used by others to attempt to contradict parts of the Bible, was one of the Bible's greatest defenders. He wrote several papers supporting the accuracy of the text and spoke out against the Bible critics of his day.

It wasn't until the confirmation nearly 200 years later of general relativity (developed by Einstein) that scientific knowledge reached the level necessary to realize the Bible is accurate in its description of time and space.

interrelated. Over many years, scientists in applied physics have conducted many tests verifying the accuracy of the concept and equations. Among many other things, several important conclusions have been drawn.[7,8]

1. That *time itself* had a beginning.

2. That *space* and *matter* had a beginning.

These two facts imply that there must have been a Creator. (For something to have a beginning, it had to have a "beginner".) In 1992, major discoveries added strong support to the idea of a "beginning" of the universe by helping define *when* and *how* the universe began (that is, the process God employed). This has had a major impact on the body of scientists who are aware of the implications. Such prominent scientists as Stephen Hawking, Carlos Frenk, and Michael Turner have considered these discoveries possible (or even likely) evidence of a Creator. Major news media gave unusual front-page and prime-time television coverage to several discoveries—highly unusual for such events.[7] Dramatically and suddenly the last hope of people committed to evolution was dealt a fatal blow (namely, the hope of an infinite universe). While Newtonian physics allowed for an infinite universe, general relativity and "big bang" evidence have disproved it.

The Bible has many places where it mentions the beginning of time and space (for example, 2 Timothy 1:9; Titus 1:2; 1 Corinthians 2:7). Tragically, it will be many *more* years before libraries and textbooks catch up with the recent discoveries.

Insights into Astronomy

The Bible indicates that the "heavens declare the glory of God" (Psalm 19:1). Such "glory" is also revealed in the Bible's many astronomical insights far ahead of human science—from the earth's shape to details about stars to the expanding universe.

The Earth Is Round

Schoolchildren are aware of misconceptions about the shape of the earth existing as late as the time of Columbus. Isaiah, speaking about 700 B.C., correctly identified the earth's shape (Isaiah 40:22). Several translations of the Bible render the Hebrew word "khug" as "circle" (still indicative of the correct shape). Some scholars believe "sphere" is a more precise interpretation of the word.

The Earth Is Suspended in Space

Ancient thought from various cultures indicates some interesting impressions of the earth. The Chinese thought the earth was square. The Egyptians thought it was rectangular with a "starry" goddess arching her body over the earth while the sun and moon massaged her arms

Are the Stars Uncountable?

At one time the world thought there were 1100 stars in the universe. In about A.D. 100 Ptolemy was actively cataloging and naming stars.

Yet the prophet Jeremiah described the stars as "uncountable" in about 600 B.C. (Jeremiah 33:22).

Astronomers now estimate there are about 100 billion stars in our galaxy and further estimate about 100 billion galaxies. If someone started counting stars at a rate of 10 per second, it would take over 100 trillion years to "count" the stars—which is obviously impossible.

and legs. Mesopotamians thought of earth as a floating boat covered by an astrodome-like structure. About 2000 B.C., the Bible indicated that the earth hangs on nothing but space (Job 26:7).

The Universe Is Expanding

Recent discoveries verify the "certainty" that the universe is expanding. Although such an idea was not popular scientifically until the twentieth century, several places in the Bible describe the concept of an expanding, or stretched-out, universe. There are references in the Psalms, written about 1000 B.C. (Psalm 104:1,2) and in Isaiah from about 700 B.C. (Isaiah 42:5; 45:12).

Every Star Is Different

Popular belief once assumed that all stars are identical. Although one Greek astronomer, Hipparchus, started classifying stars according to brightness in 125 B.C., science didn't realize how different each star was until hundreds of years later (Herschel, 1780). In the Bible, Paul emphasized the different "splendor" of stars in about 55 A.D. (1 Corinthians 15:41).

Insights into Geology

The natural processes of the earth are taken for granted today. The actions of water, air, and weather patterns are well understood. But not many years ago, the world was ignorant of much of geological science. The Bible correctly identifies several things which were later discovered.

The Hydrologic Cycle

Water comes to the earth as rain, runs down hills into rivers and back to the oceans, where it evaporates, eventually to fall as rain again. This is a simple concept, but it was not clearly recognized by science until Perrault and Mariotte correctly identified the process in the 1700s.

The Bible very precisely identifies the hydrological cycle in several places. Thousands of years before Christ, the book of Job describes the evaporation of drops of water, which are then distilled to form clouds that later pour down rain (Job 36:27,28). Ecclesiastes, written almost a thousand years before Christ, likewise describes the movement of water into streams, to the oceans, only to return to form new streams (Ecclesiastes 1:7).

Currents in the Ocean

Archaeologists have used the Bible as a trusted historical document, which has often led to discoveries of entire ancient cultures and cities. Few scientists have shared such a conviction, perhaps because the Bible was not written as a book of science. One who did, however, was Matthew Fontaine Maury. Maury reasoned that the mention of "pathways in the seas" in the book of Isaiah had to be correct (Isaiah 43:16). As a result, he spent much of his life discovering and mapping ocean currents for use

Nuclear Explosions?

How will the earth end? The Bible indicates it will be by "fire" accompanied with a "roar." It will be so violent that the earth will "be laid bare" and even "the elements will melt away" (2 Peter 3:10).

Until 1945, the world knew of nothing so horrible, so destructive. Now many people believe the spectre of nuclear holocaust provides a possible explanation for this reference.

by sailors to improve the efficiency of sea travel and to reduce accidents. His research, published in 1855, has been an invaluable

resource to the world and earned Maury the reputation as the "father of oceanography." The book of Psalms also points out the "paths in the sea" (Psalm 8:8).

Global Wind Patterns

Only with advanced satellite technology have we been able to accurately define global wind currents. Yet Ecclesiastes, written by Solomon a thousand years before Christ, describes the repeated cycle of wind blowing to the south, turning to the north, and returning in the same pattern (Ecclesiastes 1:6), though Solomon had no satellites or tools to predict global air flow.

Understanding Miracles

A miracle is defined as something unexplainable by the laws of nature, thereby requiring a supernatural cause—the involvement of God. Miracles generally fit into two categories:

1. *Miracles of Circumstance*—These are events that work within the laws of nature we know, yet are miraculous in timing or effect. An example is when God used hail to decimate the enemy during Joshua's battle against the Amorites outside of Gilgal (Joshua 10:6-11). Natural hail is not unusual, but hail directed in a way that killed the enemy and not Israel was miraculous.

2. *Miracles Beyond Known Physical Laws*—Another type of miracle is when something happens completely outside the known laws of physics. Examples are: turning water into wine (John 2:1-11); healing the lame (John 5:1-13); or feeding the multitudes with a few fish (Matthew 14:15-21).

The key to understanding miracles is recognizing that we are limited to the knowledge of the dimensions of time and space that we live in. Except in the realm of mathematics, we can only speculate about dimensions outside the four we know. And it's obviously impossible to observe any scientific laws in dimensions beyond our own. Perhaps all miracles follow some type of "natural laws" in the dimensions beyond time and space. Perhaps they don't. In either case, a God who could create the laws in the first place would certainly know how to supersede or change them.

Imagine a "3-D God"

One way to relate to the effect of the existence of extra dimensions is to imagine a world reduced to only two dimensions (like a tabletop). Imagine further the existence of several tiny "flat" human beings. The "flatpeople" would view each other as only a line. They could get an idea of the overall shape of each other only by moving around each other. They would *not* have the complete view of a three-dimensional observer.

Let's call such a three-dimensional observer "3-D God." 3-D God would be able to view an entire flatperson at once. Likewise, the 3-D God could place a finger a fraction of an inch above a flatperson, and the flatperson would never know he was there. The 3-D God would be totally invisible in the world of two dimensions unless he chose to insert himself into it. By placing a finger on the two-dimensional plane, 3-D God would appear as one line to the flatpeople. By placing three fingers on the plane, he would appear as three lines. In either case, the flatpeople would have very little concept of the totality of 3-D God. They would probably be puzzled as to how such a 3-D God could exist as both one and three lines at the same time.

Likewise, the 3-D God could know much more about a flat individual than the flatperson would know about himself or herself. 3-D God could also observe the totality of all flatpeople at once, even when the flatpeople were far apart. And 3-D God could do things that would be considered miracles in the two-dimensional world. For example, he could move a flatperson to a higher dimension, which may be called "heaven" and which would be totally imperceptible in a two-dimensional world.

Such a simple illustration provides some insight into the impact of adding only one dimension to existence. A real God existing in many dimensions outside of time and space could presumably produce far more complex miracles far more beyond our understanding.

Common Questions About Bible Events

The Bible recounts many miracles and unusual events. Even though these events are out of the ordinary, researchers have found evidence supporting their occurrence. A partial summary is below:

Can we believe the long life spans? The Bible claims early men lived to be several hundred years old—sometimes exceeding 900 years in age (Genesis 5). Ancient Babylonian writings record life spans of a similar range. Scientists believe a cataclysmic cosmic event, the Vela Supernova, occurred around the time of the great flood. This event dramatically increased cosmic radiation to the earth. This radiation is believed to be a primary cause of aging, and will continue to bombard the earth for thousands of years more.[3]

Where did Cain's wife come from? Some people wonder how Adam's sons found wives. The answer is, they came from among Adam and Eve's "other sons and daughters" (Genesis 5:4). Scholars estimate the population of earth by the time of Adam's death was in the millions. Incest was not specifically forbidden until Moses (Leviticus 20:17).[10]

Does a Hare Chew Its Cud?

A surprising statement indicating hares chew cud (which occurs only in animals with multiple stomachs) may appear to be a biblical error (Leviticus 11:5). In fact, the purpose here was *instructional*, not scientific. The appearance of a rabbit chewing is identical to that of "chewing cud"—a common, easily understood reference for people. Perhaps more to the point, the hare is unique in its practice of "refection" (at times it eats certain waste droppings) which is similar in principle to regurgitation from the stomach (chewing cud).[11]

What about the great flood? The accounts of many cultures indicate that a great flood (Genesis 6–8) occurred that wiped out humanity and much other life. It is recorded in the writings of over 200 civilizations around the world. Some scholars insist the flood was global and provide supporting evidence.[5] Others point to the specific wording of the Hebrew text of the Bible and conclude that a massive regional flood is more reasonable scientifically, yet is also completely consistent with the biblical text.[3,4]

Could the parting of the Red Sea and the Jordan River really have occurred? Were these miracles of either timing or physics? There have been historical reports of partings of the Red Sea by wind (though apparently on a much smaller scale). And earthquakes have been known to "dam up" the Jordan River as in the Bible (Exodus 14:21,22; Joshua 3:13).

What can we believe about the long day of Joshua? The Bible speaks of God's lengthening a day to assist in Joshua's defeat of the Amorites (Joshua 10:12-14). Several hypotheses have been proposed by scholars, from a slowed rotation of the earth (which would have required other miracles to avoid worldwide catastrophe) to meteorological changes having the same effect. Reports of a long day from Hindu, Chinese, and Egyptian sources seem to indicate some type of unusual worldwide event.[11,12]

Could Jonah survive in a fish? Obviously, with intervention from God, survival is *always* possible. History records that in 1891 John Bartley survived a day and a half in the belly of a whale before being rescued (this happened during a whaling expedition). In 1771 Marshall Jenkins likewise survived for a period inside a sperm whale. Sufficient interior oxygen for survival is provided by several types of whales and large fish.[10,12]

Other Common Questions

What if I Don't Believe the Entire Bible?

Having a relationship with God does not depend on your believing the entire Bible. Belief in Jesus as Savior and asking Him to be director of your life are all that is required. The entire truth of the Bible will be revealed to you over time.

Some people wonder why God uses prophecy and sometimes uses cryptic wording. There is no absolute answer to this. Perhaps God wants people to seek Him and then find Him. Perhaps He wants to emphasize faith. Or perhaps He wants to allow the Holy Spirit to reach different people in different ways. Even so, general evidence for the reliability of the Bible is also abundant.

How Can We Ensure the Right Relationship So We Can Go to Heaven?

When Jesus said not all who use His name will enter heaven (Matthew 7:21-23), He was referring to people who think using Christ's name along with rituals and rules is the key to heaven. A *relationship* with God is *not* based on rituals and rules. It's based on grace and forgiveness and the right kind of relationship with Him.

How to Have a Personal Relationship with God

1. Believe that God exists and that He came to earth in the human form of Jesus Christ (John 3:16; Romans 10:9).

2. Accept God's free forgiveness of sins through the death and resurrection of Jesus Christ (Ephesians 2:8-10; Ephesians 1:7,8).

3. Switch to God's plan for life (1 Peter 1:21-23; Ephesians 2:1-5).

4. Express desire for Christ to be director of your life (Matthew 7:21-27; 1 John 4:15).

Prayer for Eternal Life with God

"Dear God, I believe You sent Your Son, Jesus, to die for my sins so I can be forgiven. I'm sorry for my sins, and I want to live the rest of my life the way You want me to. Please put Your Spirit in my life to direct me. Amen."

Then What?

People who have sincerely taken these steps automatically become members of God's family of believers. A new world of freedom and strength is available through prayer and obedience to God's will. New believers can build their relationship with God by taking the following steps:

- Find a Bible-based church that you like and attend regularly.

- Try to set aside some time each day to pray and read the Bible.

- Locate other Christians to spend time with on a regular basis.

God's Promises to Believers

For Today

But seek first His kingdom and His righteousness, and all these things [things to satisfy all your needs] will be given to you as well.
—Matthew 6:33

For Eternity

Whoever believes in the Son has eternal life, but whoever rejects the Son will not see life, for God's wrath remains on him.
—John 3:36

Once we develop an eternal perspective, even the greatest problems on earth fade in significance.

Notes

1. McDowell, Josh, and Wilson, Bill, *A Ready Defense*, San Bernardino, CA: Here's Life Publishers, Inc., 1990.

2. Morris, Henry M., *Men of Science—Men of God*, El Cajon, CA: Master Books, 1992.

3. Ross, Hugh, Ph.D., *Noah and the Ark*, Videotape, Pasadena, CA: Reasons to Believe, 1991.

4. Ross, Hugh, Ph.D., *The Universal Flood*, Videotape, Pasadena, CA: Reasons to Believe, 1991.

5. Whitcomb, John C., and Morris, Henry M., *The Genesis Flood*, Phillipsburg, NJ: Presbyterian and Reformed Publishing Co., 1961.

6. Ross, Hugh, Ph.D., *Facts & Faith*, Pasadena, CA: Reasons to Believe, Fall, 1995.

7. Ross, Hugh, Ph.D., *The Creator and the Cosmos*, Colorado Springs, CO: NavPress, 1993.

8. Ross, Hugh, Ph.D., *The Fingerprint of God*, Orange, CA: Promise Publishing Co., 1989.

9. McMillen, S. I., *None of These Diseases*, Grand Rapids, MI: Fleming H. Revell, 1993.

10. McDowell, Josh, and Stewart, Don, *Answers to Tough Questions*, Wheaton, IL: Living Books, 1980.

11. Archer, Gleason L, *Encyclopedia of Bible Difficulties*, Grand Rapids, MI: Zondervan, 1982.

12. Stewart, Don, *The Bible and Science—Are They in Conflict?*, Spokane, WA: AusAmerica Publishers, 1993.

Bibliography

Note: The author does not agree with all authors below on all viewpoints—some of which differ with each other. Each reference has some findings worthy of consideration. DIffering viewpoints have been provided to give the reader a chance to evaluate divergent opinions.

Test everything. Hold onto the good—1 Thessalonians 5:21.

Eastman, MD, Mark, and Missler, Chuck, *The Creator Beyond Time and Space*, Costa Mesa, CA: The Word for Today, 1996.

Encyclopedia Britannica, Chicago, IL: 1993.

Free, Joseph P., and Vos, Howard F., *Archaeology and Bible History*, Grand Rapids, MI: Zondervan, 1969.

McDowell, Josh, and Stewart, Don, *Reasons Skeptics Should Consider Christianity*, Wheaton, IL : Living Books, 1981.

McDowell, Josh, and Wilson, Bill, *He Walked Among Us*, Nashville, TN: Thomas Nelson, Inc., 1993.

Missler, Chuck, *Beyond Perception*, Audiotape, Coeur d'Alene, ID: Koinonia House Inc., 1994.

Missler, Chuck, *Beyond Time & Space*, Audiotape, Coeur d'Alene, ID: Koinonia House Inc., 1994.

Morris, Henry M., and Parker, Gary E., *What Is Creation Science?* El Cajon, CA: Master Books, 1987.

Muncaster, Ralph O., *The Bible—General Analysis—Investigation of the Evidence*, Newport Beach, CA: Strong Basis to Believe, 1996.

Ross, Hugh, Ph.D., *Creation and Time*, Colorado Springs, CO: NavPress, 1994.

Smith, F. LaGard, *The Daily Bible in Chronological Order*, Eugene, OR: Harvest House, 1984.

Youngblood, Ronald F., *New Illustrated Bible Dictionary*, Nashville, TN: Thomas Nelson, Inc., 1995.